Two Percent Townsend

For my sons, Richard and Simon, daughter-in-law Lucy
and granddaughters, Esme and Clara

Crumps Barn Studio
Syde, Cheltenham GL53 9PN
www.crumpsbarnstudio.co.uk

Copyright © John Townsend 2023
Reprinted 2024

Cover design by Lorna Gray
Photographs copyright © John Townsend

All our books are printed on responsibly sourced paper from
managed woodlands and recycled material. Printed in the UK
by CMP, Poole.

ISBN 978-1-915067-29-6

Two Percent Townsend
JOHN TOWNSEND
A memoir

Crumps Barn Studio

Harry and Kate Townsend on their wedding day,
9 August 1924

EARLY DAYS

I was born on 17 March 1939, St Patrick's Day, hence my middle name Patrick. My place of birth was Yew Tree Cottage, Cold Slad Lane, Crickley Hill. The Yew tree was long gone and now, sadly, is the cottage. It was demolished some years ago. My mother would be very upset and annoyed to know her house was gone as it was built by her grandfather Eli Walker.

My great grandfather Eli was born in Coberley in 1824, and became a stone mason. His mother was later transported to Tasmania in 1830 for stealing a leg of lamb. He was famous for his propagation of a new potato called Walker's Seedling. I have a copy of his obituary from the local paper dated 1907.

My mother, Kate Walker Francis Hawker, was the third generation to live at the cottage. Her father was Thomas Hawker, born in Leckhampton, and her mother was Sarah Ann, the daughter of Eli.

My father Harry was a true Cockney, born in Stepney in 1899 to a poor family, whose father had been a self-employed wood-chopper. He came to Gloucestershire as an orphan aged 13 and was taken in by Mr Partridge of Sheepscombe, the originators of the building firm at Birdlip. My father was self-employed in the 1930s and employed two men as painters and decorators. They would all go to work, ladders and all, on an old belt driven motorbike and sidecar. These were very hard times. Just before World War II he went back to work for the Partridges at Birdlip. My mother used to say some weeks she would only have five shillings or less for housekeeping.

Born just before World War II, my memories of that time include a barrage balloon rising up every day in front of our house, based in a field next to Bentham Church. When my mother took me to town for the Thursday shop day we would go to lunch at The British Restaurant where you could have a meal for a few pence. When we came back on the bus after dark, search lights would sometimes be lighting up the sky in various directions. If the anti-aircraft guns at Nettleton were firing when we got off the bus at the Air Balloon pub, we would shelter in Mr Pearce's porch, sometimes hearing the shrapnel falling into the trees in the 'Scrubs'.

In about 1940 when the two steel lime kilns were still working at Crickley Quarries, a German bomber must have thought they were steelworks or something and dropped a load of incendiary bombs right across both sides of Crickley Hill. My Father who was an ARP man said the whole hillside was on fire. One went through the roof of Haroldstone Lodge and another into the tin bungalow at the end of the lane, but luckily, both houses were saved. Years later when my brother and I burnt the grass on the hillside, we would find the fins of the bombs and take them home. They were still in the cupboard years later.

On 14 May 1941 when I was 2 years 2 months old – the date I recently found out from a man who had worked at the Gloucester Aircraft factory – there was an awful noise coming up from below our house. My mother and our neighbours, with me following hanging on to her apron strings, ran round the hill to look down at Bentham factory but nothing was to be seen. It was some weeks before we heard that it was the testing of a new jet engine.

In late 1943, a neighbour Peter and I would stand at the railings at the end of the lane and watch large army lorries full of American troops with tanks and guns crawling up Crickley Hill. A lot of them were black and I had never seen a black man before. My cry was "got any gum chum?" and we would be rewarded with vast amounts of gum and sweets, too much for our pockets, so we had to fold up the front of our pullovers to carry our goodies home. The stone walls on the left-hand side of the hill and the walls at the end of the Air Balloon pub were ground to dust by lorries backing into them when they overheated or broke down. The same thing happened at the Birdlip T junction as the bend was too sharp for the tank trailers.

Late in the war my father was a Police Special Constable. I remember him going off in the evenings to patrol the neighbourhood.

I had two brothers, Bob who was 8 ½ years older and Charlie who was 12 years older than me. When Charlie was 17, he joined the Home Guard based in an old shed at no 1. Oxford Cottage, Ullenwood. He would come home with his .303 rifle and I remember him having a pot at a rabbit on the hill behind our house. They would go to a practice range under the bank by the peak off Birdlip Common. Later a rifle range was built at Seven Springs. After the war this was used by the rifle club with many local men involved. I have an old list of members. There was also a local squirrel shooting club in the 50s, I have a photo of them.

Our house had the electricity put in in 1939 so I never knew the age of oil lamps, unlike my wife who never had electricity until she was 12. The mains water was not taken up to Crickley Hill until 1950. We had a deep well in our garden that my father or brothers would fetch buckets of pure cold water from each morning and store it in an earthenware crock in the larder. We had no drainage, so it was chamber pots in the bedrooms and a bucket toilet out the back that had to be dug into the garden every week. Where the bucket was emptied there was always a good crop of wild tomatoes and it grew spuds 'as big as your boots'. Toilet paper was ripped up newspaper and comics apart from at Christmas when the oranges came wrapped in lovely soft tissue paper. Bath night was on Saturday in a tin bath in front of the fire. The water was heated in an old cast iron copper fireplace in the back kitchen, as it was for wash days on Monday. In later years one had to wash in a bowl of hot water, down as far as possible and up as far as possible. There was no such thing as BO in those days, everybody smelt the same. They do say too much bathing is not good for you! My mother did all the cooking on an open range with an oven on the side, she cooked in cast iron saucepans and did her ironing with flat irons heated on a bar in front of the fire. We used to riddle the ashes and use the fuel again in the back-room copper. We had a new Belling Electric cooker in 1950.

During the war and in the 1950s we always kept a pig or two, and there was always a side of bacon hanging on the kitchen wall, where one could cut off a nice thick slice of bacon for breakfast. My mother would roast pigs head and make pigs trotter stew and press chitterlings. Nothing was wasted.

In our hamlet of six houses, we lived at the top end and were the only family to own our house. My father had modernised it slightly in the 1930s with a new staircase and larder. Next to the larder, he built into the bank a semi-underground store which we called the 'tater' house, where we would store the spuds, carrots, and swedes etc. Apples were stored there too, on slatted shelves. Big green cooking apples called 'Under leaves', from a tree in the garden. They would store all winter, turning yellow and keep to April.

Sometime during the thirties, up and to the side of our cottage, my father built a rather nice summer house. It was made with tongue and groove board with a tin roof and louvre panels, tiled floor, and door on the front. It was a playhouse for me and my friends on wet days. Later I used it for keeping rabbits, ferrets and bantams, and then scrap metal. After I'd left home Charlie kept his dogs in there.

Next door, in a small two up two down, lived Mr and

Mrs Holtham. When they died my Aunty Anne Wiggle came to live there when she retired from service. She was my mother's cousin who had been adopted by my grandmother after the death of her mother and had lived at Yew Tree cottage before going into service.

Next door to her was the Gillet family who had 4 girls and a boy. They bought a television, the first in our hamlet and invited all the neighbours to watch the coronation in 1953. Next to them was the Field family, 2 boys and 2 girls, who had come over from Surrey during the war. The oldest girl Avice was to become my sister-in-law.

Down the road in a one up one down was Mr Barnfield and his wife, a real old countryman, who wore leather gaiters. He had a horse drawn plough. He would borrow a cart horse from a local farm to plough his garden every year. Dick Barnfield used to like the cider and would sit in the window at the Air Balloon pub. The cider would go straight through him and he'd stink the pub out, and Les Davis, the landlord would have to load him into his car and take him home to his poor wife. The locals called the cider 'Circus Cider' as it was three times round the ring then out!

Jack Gillet never seemed to go to work and every morning he would walk up by our cottage with his .410 shot gun under his arm and go round on the Common. I remember we teased him with 'will it kill it, Mr Gillet'. He nearly always came back carrying a rabbit. His daughter Mary would everyday go up into the Scrubs and come back dragging a load of beech logs. They seemed to live off the land. At the weekends in the winter, the Fields and I would take an old pram up to the Scrubs and come back pushing and pulling a vast load of wood to share between us.

Throughout my younger days we had most of our daily groceries delivered. Bread from Townsend's bakery at Shurdington, and milk from Sam Hewinson's Dairy at Dry Hill Farm that came in thick pint bottles with a round cardboard stopper. I would sometimes go with Sam to help and deliver to Ullenwood Camp when the Americans were there. Papers were delivered by Mr Joe Patrick and meat from Nash and Co. the Strand in Cheltenham. The post was delivered by Mrs Hunt from Witcombe who walked up the hill and round the lane with a large leather bag six days a week in all weathers. Mr Lusty came on Saturdays in an old bus and sold paraffin, soap, tinned food, and tins of biscuits and about anything you wanted including bottles of Tizer at 9d with 3d back when returning the bottle. My mother would go shopping on Thursdays, going to the Co-op in the high street, where sugar, tea and rice were weighed into blue paper bags. At the end of the year, she would collect her dividend money for Christmas.

One evening during the war we saw, from home, a massive blaze on Birdlip Common. My brothers went up there and saw a lorry, loaded with about ten tonnes of sugar, on fire. The sugar was in 7lb tins on a flat-bed held on with tarpaulin and ropes. The corner of the tarpaulin was burnt through and the tins were falling off and rolling down the hill, some were scorched on the outside and inside, under a layer of toffee, there was pure white sugar. All the locals were helping themselves to the tins. My brothers came home and got my old pram and came back with it filled up. Sugar was rationed so it came in very handy. It tasted a little burnt but was okay for puddings etc. It lasted us a couple of years.

When I was about 5 years old, my brother Charlie worked at Crickley Farm at the foot of the hill, the house and buildings are now covered by the new road. After milking, Charlie would go with a horse and cart and set gin traps, about a hundred or more, and next day go and pick up the rabbits. I can remember him coming back with as many as 75 rabbits laid in the cart all swaying to its motion. Mr Millard the farmer would sell them to the War Agricultural for about a shilling each.

We had a grey and white cat, named Cheetah after Tarzan's ape. She would produce two litters of kittens a year, in a box put out for her in the summer house. Her kittens were multi-coloured and unusually had six claws, fathered by a semi feral black and white cat with the same. It had been left behind by the Field family when they moved. We always managed to find a home for the kittens, one even going to America. Cheetah would often come home with a rabbit almost as big as herself. Sadly one day she didn't come home, and although we searched for her, we never saw her again.

About that time Pat Smythe and her parents came to live at Crickley, renting Crickley Lodge which was below our house. Pat was to become a very famous show jumper in the 50s. My brother Bob used to milk their Jersey cow in the field next to their house. At this time, they stabled their horses at the Royal George at Birdlip. Her mother had an old army jeep, and I would sometimes go with them to Cheltenham Gas works to buy coke for their boiler, helping them fill the sacks. Her mother was later killed in her jeep at Slad, when she skidded on the ice and turned over on a bend.

By the time I was 5, my brother Bob had already left school at Birdlip and on my first day there, I was taken by my neighbour Rosy Gillet. I already had a best friend, Alan Holtham whose grandparents had come to live next door in the war time, and we used to play together when his parents visited. Birdlip school was idyllic, my six years there were very instructive. The infant's class was in the old wooden village hut, heated by an old coke stove. We were taught the alphabet with sand-boards, our teachers were Miss Payne, Mrs Cambridge, and Mrs Coxhead, but I cannot remember the order they came in.

In the bad winter of 1947, we had a very deep snow and did not go to school for quite a few weeks. When we returned, we were walking level with the top of the stone walls on the frozen snow. It was some weeks before it was dug out by hand by the local men. In the summer we would go on nature walks, learning the names of plants and flowers, gathering them to take back and draw.

Everyday two boys would be sent over to Mr Parson's farm to collect a crate of milk that was straight from the cow, not pasteurised like today. In the summer we would go over to Parsons's farm and play rounders, trying to avoid the cow pats which the ball always seemed to land in.

Moving up to the Juniors in the old stone schoolhouse, heated again by an old coke stove, Mrs Davis who lived in the village, was our teacher, quite stern but fair. I cannot remember her ever smiling. We were joined at Birdlip by all the children from Brimpsfield School when it closed, and we made some good friends. Terry Fry, Brian James, Arthur and Natty Partridge and Dicky Juggins to name a few.

Terry Fry was the class comedian, he would blow raspberries on his arm making all laugh only to be called up by Mrs Davis for a few whacks on the arm with a ruler. Most of us would get the ruler quite often, even the girls. The boy's toilet at Birdlip School consisted of a concrete wall with a drain at one end. The boys would stand in line and see who could pee the highest. There was a small wooden seat with a bucket underneath. One morning I went there on my own and on the spur of the moment I wrote 'poo' on the wall with a piece of chalk I had in my pocket. Sometime later someone told Mrs Davis. She produced pieces of paper and gave one to all the boys and asked us to write poo on it. Knowing what she was at I wrote 'pooh' on my paper and quickly got rid of the piece of chalk in my desk. She never found out who it was, and I saved myself a caning.

About 1946 we were joined by three families who lived in the huts on the gun sight at Nettleton. They were families who had been bombed out of their homes elsewhere. The locals called them Squatters. They were the Kents, Wests and the Birkenheads.

The boys' favourite book at Birdlip School was a large red book on the top shelf about British birds and their eggs. If we were good Mrs Davis would let us look at it, we all collected bird's eggs in those days. The school had four garden plots where in summer we would dig, plant and nurture and clip the grass paths. Mrs Davis would watch us out of the window and woe betide anyone who pinched a strawberry or anything else. The veg would disappear overnight, picked by her and her husband. When Alan and I became the eldest boys, she would send us up to Beechwood to gather pea sticks armed with a billhook and pieces of string, we would make that last all morning. While the boys were gardening the girls would have sewing lessons, sometimes sitting outside if it was sunny.

I had a small lead cannon that fired matchsticks and was playing with it on my desk. I was going to shoot it at Terry Fry in the window, but I slipped, and it landed on Mrs Davis's desk. "Who did that" she cried. I kept quiet but some twitty girl said "John Townsend!" Mrs Davis marched up, made me hand it over, and promptly put it in the coke stove saying, "let that be a lesson to you". I was so annoyed to lose my cannon that I poked my tongue out at her, only to receive a good hiding with the ruler.

My neighbours, Peter and Barbera Field and I were picked up at the end of Cold Slad Lane in the morning by Mr Gifford. He had a taxi service from the house next to the Royal Hotel at Birdlip. He drove a Ford V8 Pilot car and was nearly always late. After going round the bend at the Air Balloon he would accelerate up over the common, much encouraged by us, up to 90 miles an hour or so, only having to break sharply outside Birdlip to avoid Mrs Willis's cows coming out from milking. Mr Gifford had three sons at Birdlip School, Derek, Cedric and Tony. We went home on the 3.00pm bus but if it was fine, we walked across the fields from the school to the Cuckoo Pen then over the Birdlip Common and down over through Grove Farm to Slad Lane. Any pennies we saved we could spend in Birdlip shop.

Terry Fry liked to give everyone a nickname, my name was 'Trow' or 'Trousers', partly from my surname and the fact that I always had a patch in the back of my short trousers, caused by sliding down the grassy banks on Crickley Hill. Alan was called 'Ass-legs' because of his narrow waist and broad shoulders. Dicky Juggins was called 'Buggins' but not to his face or you would get a slap. Brian was called 'simply Jamer'. Terry was called 'Frisby Dyke', but I won't go into how he got his name.

The school wall looked down onto the main road, anything or anybody going by resulted in a line of faces looking down. One of our favourites was Herbie Ludlow from Catchbar. He wasn't quite the 'full quid', and we would say, "where you bin Herbie?" and he would say, "I've bin to see Mr Partridge, him's no bloody good!". Another attraction was Charlie Hudder who had very large feet and would pass by on his bike with his feet stuck out at 90 degrees, much to our amusement. The locals called him 'ten to two'. He was later to become the major bust of local policeman, Ken Hudman, when he booked him for having no lights on his bike. There would also be convoys of soldiers coming home from the war and we would line up and wave to them.

When we were 10, we took the 11 plus exam, I found it quite easy. My mate Alan sat behind me in the back row, and I tried to help him, but he didn't pass. Later, I wished I hadn't either. From an early age Alan and I would hang around the local farms, if it were hay making time, we were quickly given a fork each and we would help to turn, cock or rick the hay, we were never paid or asked to be, because come harvest time we followed the binders, and because we were helpful they didn't mind. We were after the rabbits!

I joined the Cubs when I was 8 years old, we used to meet at Beechwood House, the home of Miss Butlers, Ruth was our Cub Mistress. My school friend Ian Hoskins lived there also. We learnt a lot of skills and had good fun. Later, I was in the scouts 23rd Cheltenham. We used to meet at the hut in Birdlip. The two senior scouts were Derek Beard and Michael Manners, plus all the Birdlip boys. One year I went on a scout camp by train to a place called Timbercombe in Somerset, where we walked over the hills to Minehead and splashed about in a local stream. We cooked over a campfire and made cakes from flour and water called Damper, which we fried over the fire.

I was out with my friend Ian Hoskins in the Scrubs and we found a young jay that had fallen from its nest,

I took it home and reared it on a diet of bread, fruit and insects. Arriving home from school days it would hop onto my shoulder and go everywhere with me. It was my constant companion for about 3 months. It lived in an outside washroom. Sadly, it was killed when a heavy bicycle crank fell on it.

Charlie aged 14, Bob aged 10, and the author aged 14 months

My best mate, Alan Holtham

At Birdlip School

Scout camp at Timbercombe, Somerset

*With Rosy Gillet, Avice and Bob at Miss Butler's
house for a scout do*

Local men digging snow off the roads in Birdlip in 1947

Squirrels shooters (left to right): Bob Partridge, Jack Beard (my father-in-law), Bill Adams, Alan Wilson, Eric Hodges, George Beard, [unknown], John Wilson, Jack Gillet (with his 4.10) and Wilf Tibbles

CHURN VALLEY RIFLE CLUB

NAMES.		No of attendances		
Andrews.	T.D.H.	1	GEGG. R	2
BARNFIELD	W.	7.	GILLEF...	2
BEARD.	W.J.	8.	GOLDING. W.J.	1
BEARD	G.	5.	HARRISON P.J.S.	1
BEARD	J.H.	3	HAYES. R.C.	4
BEARD	A.	1	HAWARD. W.	2
BLISS.	R.J.	1	HOLDER A.E	2
BLOWEN	G	1	HOPWOOD H.	4
BLOWEN	T.	1	HULL. W.	1
BRUNSDEN	E	3	HARRIS. H.N.G.	2
CAMERON	J.	1	HAWARD A.N	1
CARPENTER	J.	5	HELEY P	1
CHAMBERLAIN	A.	5	JONES. A.P	6.
CLARK	H.J.	6	KENDALL J.N	4
CLAYTON	J	2	LEACH J.	1
COLLETT.	J.	2	MITCHELL W	1
COLLINS	P.J.	2	MANSELL W.J	4
CARPENTER	R.	3	PARTRIDGE B	3
COOK.	J.R.W	1	PARTRIDGE H.C.	3
COOKE	W.A.	7.	PARTRIDGE M.J.	7.
DAVIS	H	3	PARTRIDGE N.J.C.	1
DAVIS	R.G.H.	3	PARTRIDGE R.H	7.
DAVIS.	F	1	PARTRIDGE C.M.	3
EDDOLS	G.	1	PRICE H.T.	1
EDMONDS.	J.	3	PRICE J.	4
FINCH	A.A.	1	PREDDY E	1
FORD.	H.F	2	PLUMBE R	1
FRANCES	E.F.C	7	PARKER W.B	1
GARLIC	G.W	1	PEARCE E	1
GILES.	F.	1	PERRY F	3
GARN	W.	6.	PRICE W.R	5

REISS	P.	1	SPENCER F.	3.
REYNOLDS.	G.	2	TOWNSEND F.G.	3
ROBERTS	C.	5	TROTMAN J.	2
PHIPS	J.	1	TWINNING A	1
RENSHAW	C.M.	1.	TWINNING F	1
SAUNDERS.	P	6	TWINNING S	5
SCUTT.	A.	1	UNDERWOOD. C.J.	5
SMITH.	E.A	5	WATTS. W	6.
SMITH	F	2	WHITMAN R.	2
SMITH	W.	8		
			Total -	81

Churn Valley Rifle Club members 1945 Seven Springs Range

Birdlip Platoon 'B' Company 3rd Glos Batt Home Guard 1943. Charlie in the 4th row, twelve from left

RABBITING DAYS

In the summer holidays Alan and I would follow the binders harvesting. I would leave home early in the morning with my sandwiches and a bottle of water saying to my mother, "I'll see you tonight at dusk". Walking up over Birdlip Common and across Stockwell Farm the sky would be full of skylarks singing away. Something you don't see today with modern farming and an over population of badgers.

When following the binder, the rabbits would squat along the edges of the corn, too frightened to run out. Alan and I, armed with a stout nut stick with an empty cartridge case stuck on one end, would clobber any rabbit we saw. When it came to the last uncut strip across the field, rabbits would be running everywhere. Some fields had a hundred or more rabbits in them. A favourite field was Mr Dickenson's three-cornered patch by Birdlip peak. Some days we might have as many as six each and our sticks we would notch for every kill. My mother was always glad when I arrived home with a few rabbits. As a child I think we lived on rabbit – boiled, roasted or stewed, it was a staple diet for many families. Mr Payne at Stockwell farm was very mean and would only let us have one each so if we could, we would hide some and pick them up later on the way home. We would hang up the skins to dry on the back wall of our house; a man would come round from town and give a few pence for them.

When we were not harvesting, I would walk up to Alan's, he lived at Castle Cottage in Nettleton about 4 miles by road or less over land as the crow flies. We spent our days wandering for miles around. I always carried a rabbit net and if we found a wall with long grass and bushes, we would set a net at one end then go back and tap along the grass, any rabbits would run along into the net.

When I was about 8 years old my brother Charlie came home with a dog he been given by Cooks, farmers at Bentham. It had arrived there as a stray, and they reckoned it had belonged to the Gypsies. He must have been about 8 years old, a Lurcher type, well built with long legs, white all over with a black spot over his eye, we called him 'Spot'. He took to me straight away and was my constant companion, the best rabbiting dog you could ever wish for. My mother would say we could do with a rabbit for tea tomorrow, so off Spot and I would go, round on the hill and seldom failed to get one. He would stand on one side of a blackberry bush while I stamped on the other side, out came a rabbit and he seldom missed it. He knew if there was a rabbit in a stone wall or hollow tree. Round at the quarries there were lots of sheets of corrugated tin lying around and we would place a stone under them for the rabbits to lie under. Lifting a corner, he would dive in quick as lightening.

Down at Cook's farm at Bentham, run by Mrs Cook and her three sons, they made a lot of cider every year. It was the gathering place for all the local characters at the weekend, farm workers, road men and builders etc. If there was any work to be done on the farm, haymaking or gathering sheaves, etc. they would all pitch in to help, after which they would all sit in the cider house, they called it the 'Ramping cat', sometimes there would be ten or twelve men sitting around on sacks. The cider house had a double row of 120-gallon barrels of cider, there was just one old horn tot to drink out of. As a young boy, if I arrived down there, they would shout "tot out boy". I would fill the tot from the barrel in use and hand it up to the first in line, it was almost a full-time job, by the time I got to the last one it was time to go around again. I liked to listen to all the old tales they had to tell.

It was at Cook's farm that I first drove a tractor when I was about 8 years old. When they were pitching hay or sheaves onto a cart, I would sit on the old Fordson Standard and move from heap to heap very carefully not to pitch them off the load.

Around the lane from my house there was a quarry, in the 20s and 30s vast amounts of gravel was excavated by Packers Ltd of Gloucester. They built two large steel lime kilns, and lorries would take the gravel and lime to Gloucester and come back with loads of slack coal for the kilns. They used old Sentinel Steam wagons. My brother always said that two old wagons were buried in a tip under the old waste lime heaps.

When my friend Alan or another friend came to my house the quarry was our playground. There were old machines to climb on, gravel slopes to slide down on sheets of tin and old lime heaps to ride over on our bikes. If Mrs May the unofficial caretaker who lived in the house below saw us, she would ring the local policeman at Birdlip. We could usually hear him coming on his motor bike and we would try to find a place to hide. Alan and I decided to make a good hiding place. We found a round 100-gallon metal tank that leaked behind the cowshed at the Air Balloon pub and rolled it about half a mile through the Scrubs to the top of the hill. Seeing nobody was about, we rolled it over the cliffs and down into the quarry. If you now go along Cold Slad lane to the Quarry there is a new gate blocking the old road, to the right of this there is a large mound, on top of this we dug a hole and buried the tank on its side and put turf over it. This was our hidey-hole. I looked a couple of years ago and it's still there seventy odd years later.

The Devil's Table, Crickley Hill

The Cook Family at Bentham

GRAMMAR SCHOOL

When I was eleven, off I went to Cheltenham Grammar School for Boys, which was down the lower High Street, next door to the Brewery. A gothic looking building with a tower and steps leading up to the front door that only the masters and sixth form could use. Lesser mortals had to use the side gate. I hated the place from the very first day. My classroom was 2C, it was dark, north facing and only a few yards from the brewery. The fumes from malted barley wafted into our classroom all day and made me feel quite ill. There I was, a country lad, in a classroom full of town kids, a fish out of water.

Our form master was Mr Parr who taught French, an evil looking man with a mortarboard and black gown. I think he took an instant dislike to me and my broad Gloucestershire accent. He called me a country bumpkin. Later that year I was reading French from a book, which unlike German doesn't read as it looks, this country bumpkin purposely read it as it looked. Mr Parr, with his mortarboard, jumping up and down, his arms waving his gown like a demented bat, called me everything under the sun. My reply, in as broad an accent as I could say, was "that's what it sez yer". He never asked me to read from a book again. At the end of the year French exam I got 2 marks out of a hundred and for the rest of my time at the school everybody called me 2% Townsend.

At the Grammar school, if you weren't good at sports you were considered rubbish. At cricket I couldn't bowl, bat or catch, at rugby I seemed to be always fullback, shivering cold while all the play was in the middle. On two occasions, while trying to scoop up the ball some idiot tried to kick it, ending with my hand swelling like a bunch of bananas, not my idea of fun, or sliding around in the mud with my head stuck up someone's dirty backside in the scrum. This resulted in me being absent, especially on games days, up to twenty days a term. I would say I was ill or missed the bus, anything to stay away from that awful school, getting further behind with my lessons. I also hated homework, I wanted to be out and about in the fields.

My best subjects were History, Geography and Woodwork which says something about my future career. I still have an oak coffee table I made at school by my bed.

Going to that school was the biggest mistake of my life. My poor mother had spent a fortune on uniform and games kit. I am sure it would have been better if I had gone to a technical school. I had to walk a mile to catch the bus to town at the Air Balloon bus stop which was always full. Two lads that were from the farm at Ullenwood used to get on, their mother never gave them handkerchiefs and they always had candles under their noses, which made me feel quite sick.

Opposite the school was a greengrocer called Stubs. For two weeks before Christmas I used to take as much mistletoe as I could carry and get seven shillings and sixpence a day. Alan and I would go down the banks below Crickley on the weekend, climb trees to pick it and would share the money. In those days mistletoe never grew anywhere in the Cotswolds above three hundred feet from the sea level, although lately I have started to see the odd piece growing around my area.

When I was about 14, a man called Dennis Blunt who had a scrap yard at Leckhampton station called on my brother Charlie. Charlie was now working as a roadman for Gloucestershire Council and would collect pieces of metal from the roadside, filling a scrap bag he had in the shed. Dennis would come every few months in an old Morris 8 Tourer and with his scales would weigh up the metal and lots of pound notes would change hands. Watching these transactions, I said to my mate Alan there's money to be made in old metal, so we went round the old tips looking for brass, copper, lead etc. A very good source was a tip at the Cuckoo Pen, outside Birdlip, where Partridges the builders tipped their waste. After a while we had several bags of metal. The next time Dennis came and had finished his transaction with my brother, I said that I had some metal for him. They said, "where have you been getting this from, you little buggers?" On weighing it up he gave me eleven pounds fifteen shillings, an absolute fortune to us. This was the start of my dealing days, from that day on I always had money in my pocket.

After four years at Cheltenham Grammar School and never above third from the bottom of my class I had had enough! Brother Charlie said Mr Yarnold at Grove Farm was looking for a lad to work for him on the farm. I went to see him, and he said, "You can start tomorrow if you like, the wages are thirty-four shillings a week for 47 hours."

I was fifteen on the 17th of March. I went to see the headmaster and said I am leaving on Friday sir, he said you can't leave until you're 16. I said sir I have a job and I start next Monday.

Only one master wished me luck, Mr Smith who taught German, his nickname was 'Pimp' owing to a large lump on his neck. He had been in the First World War as a pilot and he told us some fantastic stories. He was, compared to most of the others, a very nice man. On the last day I walked out of the front door and threw my cap with my name on it back up the corridor. No one ever came after me for leaving, I think they were glad to get rid of me. I had not been a disruptive pupil, I just spent four years mostly staring out of the window wishing to be outside in the fresh air.

One lad called Ramon Betteridge was in my class at school for the first three years. I didn't know him very well until his family moved up to Nettleton, to live in the small cottage just above the Golden Heart. The cottage is now gone, pulled down when they altered the road. I used to meet up in Birdlip with Alan, Ray and Terry. Ray was a very cheeky lad. One night we were cycling in Cranham woods and saw a courting couple down in a quarry, naked in the back of a car. Ray crept down and took the man's clothes off the front of the car seat and ran. He was chased through the wood by a naked man picking up clothes bit by bit, it was so funny.

Ray joined the police force as a cadet when he was sixteen, then the family moved away, and I never saw him again. Then one day in the 1970s he turned up with his wife Colleen at my store. I knew him straight away and said, "where have you been?"

It turned out that he had also been a Military Policeman (as had I in my National Service) and had had a top posting to SHAPE the NATO headquarters in Paris. He said he had often seen General Montgomery who would stop and speak to the MPs on the door and was a very nice man. After doing his National Service his family had emigrated to the USA and lived in Washington State. We've kept in touch ever since, writing at Christmas. We have recently heard that sadly he passed away in September 2020.

Aunty Anne, Mother and me at Weston-super-mare
c. 1951

FARMERS BOY

I went to work at Grove farm for Mr Yarnold, known as Boss Yarnold. The farm was about 75 acres of sloping grass land and a standing of Larch wood on the hill. Mr Yarnold was slightly built and always wore corduroy trousers with brown boots and leggings. He had about twenty-five horses ranging from cart horses to hunters and ponies and was very well known in the horsey world, riding with the Cotswold hunt. He kept two milking cows, a range of various calves and a beef herd of fifteen to twenty. He said I have a nice little job for you to start with – clean out the calves shed. Opening the shed door, the calves were standing almost above my head on about five feet of muck. It took me about a week between other jobs to shovel the muck out through a window.

I had to clean, feed, muck out any horses in the stables and feed the calves twice a day. Some days, if he was going out, I had to hand milk the cows taking some milk up to the house and feeding the rest to the calves.

In the small barn there was a roller mill and chaff cutter run from an electric motor and once a week I would mill oats and beans and mix with chaff and molasses to feed the animals. Boss showed me how to harness the cart horse into the cart and I would take hay up over the hill to feed the beef herd and horses.

Boss lived in the bungalow above the yard with his daughter Joyce and son-in-law Jack Garlic, who was a builder and an engineer. Almost the first week Boss asked if I would go with Jack and help him lay a concrete path. The path was from Lionel Gibbs' (the Saddler) front gate to his front door. The last time I walked down Birdlip street it was still there. Over the years I helped Jack on many jobs around the farms, a dryer at Stockwell farm, piggery at Black Lanes and a Silo at Birdlip farm. These years taught me a lot about building work. Jack was an expert welder and used the law of the lever to raise beams etc., he was a very clever man. It made a change from farm work and when I worked for him, I was paid a little extra.

Jack had built some caravans on old lorry chassis and put them up on the hill. He would advertise them up in the Midlands and we would get a lot of people from Birmingham stay for a week. One day when I was milking, two young lads looking in the door asked in a very broad 'Brummie' accent, "What you doing, Mr?" I said I was getting milk for their breakfast tomorrow. They said, "Nah, our milk comes in bottles."

Boss had an old Standard Fordson that I would have to start on the handle. Hard work for a fifteen-year-old! I would take it up near the house to a large wood pile and drive with a belt an old cast iron saw bench to saw firewood for the house, no health and safety in those days.

Some months after starting work Burgis from Gloucester arrived in their lorry with two shiny new tractors and taking the old Fordson away. They were a David Brown 30D with a mill loader and a rotavator on the back and a Davis brown 25D with a mid-mounted grass mower. As soon as I was sixteen I could drive on the road with L plates. Boss would send me out contracting for other farmers, mowing and rotavating. I have recently found an old postcard showing a mown field behind the Air Balloon pub that must have been taken the day or the day after I had mowed it.

Rotavating was quite new on the market. Arriving at English Rose gardens Hucclecote, I turned a two-acre patch of brambles into a fine tilth in a morning, much to the amazement of Mr English the owner. Grove Farm under the slopes of Birdlip Common was always known for its vast rabbit population, the farm was north facing, the yard in the valley never saw the sun after midday in the winter. The steep banks under Birdlip Common would hold a frost all day.

I could never understand how these banks were so popular with rabbits. When I went up over the hill with the horse and cart the ground would move with thousands of them. Boss would sometimes send me out with an old twelve bore and two cartridges, and woe betide me if I didn't come back with at least two rabbits. Sometimes you could get two with one shot. He would cook them in an old boiler with oats to feed two hound puppies that he walked for the Cotswold hunt.

In the summer of 1955, the rabbit disease, myxomatosis, arrived at Grove Farm, there were dead rabbits everywhere, and the smell and flies were awful.

Boss said go up on the hill and burn or bury every one you can, it took me about two weeks, there were black ones and sandy ones and in places hardly a yard between them, like a vast battle field. I would gather wood and start a fire and collect them up with a four-grain fork. I disposed of thousands and it was over a year before I saw a live rabbit again, when I was seventeen and shot one with my newly acquired .22 rifle. By then rabbit was very much off the menu for most people and still is. Very sad as they were a staple diet throughout the war years.

One evening in the spring of 1955 Mr Warner, a farmer from Little Shurdington came up to my house, he said his tractor driver had left him suddenly and he couldn't drive a tractor, did he think Boss Yarnold would lend me to him to do his haymaking? Boss said, "Why don't you have your two weeks holiday?", so off I went down over the banks every day. Mr Warner had a grey Ferguson with mower, turner and bailer. We were lucky with the weather, so in the two weeks I cut, turned and bailed and put it in his barn. I enjoyed doing it and had double wages.

Boss had a very dry sense of humour, one day after I had rotovated a patch of ground below his house, he came out with a large bag of broad beans and said plant these and fill this patch. I asked how to plant them. He said with a line and a dibber and when you have finished you will know how many beans makes five. It took me about two days to plant the half acre plot and when I was finished I said to him, "well how many beans do make five?". He said, "two in each hand and one up your a***!".

He always had a bevy of young girls in jodhpurs along on Saturday mornings to have free rides on his horses. Two local girls were Maureen Smith from Leckhampton and Beryl Bailey from Birdlip Hill who made Saturday morning work quite entertaining, also a young lad called Terry Biddlecombe soon to become a famous jockey.

Boss had some land down on the Severn called the Leigh, we would take some of his beef herd down for summer grazing. One year after some very heavy rain it flooded, we went down with his Bedford cattle lorry with a horse on board so he could ride out and bring them home.

I had a couple of near misses while working at Grove farm. Once when the horse and cart bolted and went from top to bottom down a steep bank and through a gate at an angle, with me hanging on for dear life, and again with a tractor and trailer one very frosty morning I slid sideways down a very steep bank.

Driving down to the Leigh one day when I was sixteen and a half, I said to the Boss that I was going to buy a vehicle. He asked how can you afford that on my £3 a week? I said out of the money I made from my scrap dealing and carrying it home on my bike. I bought two old US Army jeeps from Nattie Partridge at the Golden Heart Inn, in Nettleton, for forty-nine pounds and spent two months swapping the good bits to make one and painting it.

In 1956, the Suez invasion was going on and for some

reason unbeknown to me you could drive on L plates without a qualified driver with you. So on 17 March 1956 all taxed and insured, I went off and taught myself to drive on local roads. I towed home an old car, cut it up, and made a trailer. Jack welded up a tow bar for me. My dealing business really took off. I would go round all the local farmers I knew and buy stone troughs, staddle stones and scrap metal. I was very soon making more money nights and weekends that I earnt on the farm. I was now on a five-day week and on Saturday mornings I took loads of scrap to Dennis Blunt's scrap yard at Leckhampton station. I had a display of stoneware outside my house selling to people who came up Cold Slad lane to visit the Common. Staddle stones and troughs were making about £5 each at the time.

Coming up to eighteen, the Boss asked if I would like him to get me deferred from National Service. I said no as I wanted to go and see the world. Coming eighteen Boss said I can't afford to pay you anymore money as I would have to pay a man's wage, but Jack wants to take you on full time, so I left the farm and was replaced by a lad called Tony Baxter from Ullenwood. I really enjoyed my three years on the farm, pay was low, but money wasn't everything. I worked for Jack Garlic for about a year and knowing that my call-up was due anytime, in the spring of 1958 I went self-employed doing a mixture of jobs, sometimes with brother Charlie hedge trimming and walling and a lot of scrap dealing. I wasn't called up until I was nineteen and a half, on 8 October 1958. It was about this time that my friend Alan and his mother moved to Bristol. I never saw him again and sometime after he committed suicide, gassing himself in a van he had acquired. His father had taken his own life some years earlier at Castle Cottage.

From an early age, being around the farms, I was quite partial to a glass of cider. Starting work and having money to spend I would go to the back of the Air Balloon Inn and buy a quart bottle of GL Gloster Cider, costing 2/6 and 3d on the bottle, which lasted me a few evenings. Also, when about sixteen or seventeen, and not allowed in the pub I would stand outside and get somebody to buy me a drink. About this time the Americans were back at Ullenwood Camp, something to do with the Cold War and radar, and a number of them would walk along to the pub in the evening. They always wanted to buy drinks for me and my brother Charlie who would tell them some stories, a good many he would make up. Charlie would sit in the porch selling rabbits he'd caught and flowers and vegetables out of his garden.

Boss Yarnold and Jack Garlic with family

Postcard of The Severn Valley from the rear of the Air Balloon

TEENAGE YEARS

I never had a proper bike of my own until I was eleven, just before going to Cheltenham Grammar School. It took all the money from my Building Society account, £12 for a new Raleigh. Alan, Terry and I would cycle for miles around places like Wainlodes Hill on the River Severn. Later when I was sixteen or so Terry and I would cycle to Winstone to meet the girls there. One evening we went down to Cranham and made friends with a whole gang of girls and boys. When I was seventeen I bought a new motorbike, a Triumph Cub off road model. About then Mrs Emerson, the wife of the local bobby, started up a youth club at Birdlip village hall. Her daughter is the mother of 'Eddie the Eagle'. The Cranham boys came over and all the Birdlip boys and girls around attended, and we had a riotous time. Dress for me was black jeans, T-shirt and casual jacket – very James Dean. We had barbeques in Cranham Caves and on Shurdington Hill. If you could go down the caves now you would find our names written on the ceiling in candle smoke. The caves were blocked off in the sixties.

PC Emerson organised an outing to Yorkley in the Forest of Dean, where he had once been stationed, from the George Hotel. Yorkley was a village on a steep hill with eight pubs. On the way up the aim was to have a pint at each one, not many made it to the top.

In September 1956, I had owned my jeep for six months. You had to have the company of a licenced driver with you, so I took my L plates off and said I had passed my test and carried on driving.

At the youth club we would listen to the new Elvis Presley records on an old winding gramophone. After youth club Mrs Emerson liked to go down to the Golden Heart or the Green Dragon so I used to take her in the jeep and the rest would follow on their motorbikes. Nobody worried if you weren't eighteen in those days. Mrs Emerson would play the piano and sing the 'laughing policeman' and other songs, she certainly was a jolly old stick. Years later when PC Emerson had retired and had a pub in Cheltenham he told me he knew I hadn't had a full driving licence, but his wife had said, "Leave him alone he's the only one with a vehicle to take me to the pub."

Some evenings myself, Rex Taylor, Mike Cuttell, Lee Powis and Ken Baker, who all had jeeps, would line them up in the Air Balloon car park. The locals used to say Hey-up the US army's here. Les Davis the landlord of the Air Balloon was the best landlord for miles around and people used to come from all over and the pub was packed by 9 o'clock at night.

Every year he would organise a coach from Marchants for a pub outing going to places like London, Southend, Blackpool, and the Isle of Wight. The most memorable one for me was going to Bristol and going by sea on the

Bristol Queen paddle steamer to Ilfracombe. I stood on the prow drinking cans of Forest Brown Ale. The sea was quite rough; it was going up and down with the swell, I loved it, some of the others went quite green.

The 1950s for me were idyllic years, I never had a serious girlfriend apart from Susan Handcock who lived on Crickley Hill. We would meet outside her house most weeks and occasionally I took her to the cinema in Cheltenham. I went out with lots of girls from Birdlip, Cranham, Winston and Whiteway, nothing serious just a kiss and cuddle.

All my friends had guns and we had plenty of places to go shooting. You could carry a gun on your back and nobody worried. We also went fishing and swimming in various places. Cranham had a lake, very cold but clean water.

After getting motorbikes, all the other lads and I would meet up at the Black Horse pub at Cranham. Tony Baxter, Jimmy Beatson, Dennis Lewis, Mickie Davis, Cyril Mustoe, Pat Causon, Geoff Cross, Ivan George, Ken Bartlett and Brian Waldon. We all had English bikes and hated Japanese Hondas, we called them cocoa tin death traps. Roly Merideth the landlord would let us use the snug on the side, now part of the main pub. We would be joined by the local girls Anne Pratt, Margaret Regan, Pauleen Causon, Angela Monk to name a few. They were all farm and building lads and never had much money. My bits of dealing were quite lucrative, and I always had money to spare and would often push the boat out for a round. We would play cards for pennies and play spoof for 3d bars of chocolate. Drinking soft drinks and bottles of light ale, a pound note would go a long way in those days.

In the summer of 1957 myself, Cyril, Mike, Pat, Tony and Dennis went on five motorbikes for a two-week camping holiday along the south coast from Brighton to Plymouth and up to Weston-Super-Mare. We carried two tents, blankets, cooking items, food and fishing tackle all on our backs or strapped to our bikes. We caught fish and crabs and cooked them over a campfire, I made damper cakes from my scouting days. It was quite a wet time, we would lie in our tents, steam rising from our wet clothes. We all agreed it was the best holiday we ever had.

On the night before I went to do my National Service we had a party in the snug at the Black Horse. All my friends were there, we were playing three card brag when in walked two policemen from Painswick and booked us for playing cards for money, there was 3d on the table, and some for drinking underage. There was a big row in the village, the locals said we were well behaved and caused no trouble so in the end the charges were dropped. I went in the army the next day. When I came home two years later some of my friends had moved and I never saw them again.

Camping with our bikes

*Les and Irene Davis, landlord and landlady of the
Air Balloon Inn*

Postcard of Inkerman Barracks

Passing out parade

NATIONAL SERVICE

After four years on the farm and doing building work, my height and strength had increased considerably. I was now a half inch off six foot and twelve and a half stone. Some months previously my mate Dennis and I had been called to go to Gloucester for a medical, standing in line and doing the cough etc. We then had to do an exam or intelligence test. The NCO asked us which regiment we would like to go into. We both said the tank regiment, when our papers arrived I was to go to Carlisle and Dennis to Catterick.

Getting on the train at Cheltenham with my travel warrant and changing trains at Rugby, I arrived at Carlisle to join the Armour Car Regiment the 11th Hussars with their brown berets. It was quite a small intake; we were all in one hut. After being issued with our kit we were soon introduced to the square and lined up and marched around. I thought things were going quite well until a chap called Smithy and I were told to report to the CO who told us we had volunteered to be Military Policemen. I objected and said that I didn't want to be an MP, but he said you are too big to drive armoured cars so off you go, so within two weeks of going to Carlisle, Smithy and I were on the train to London through the underground and then on a train to Woking in Surrey.

On arriving at Inkerman barracks, the training centre for MPs, we were told to stand in line, about ninety of us, shortest at one end tallest at the other. We were then split into three squads 714, 715 and 716. Being 5 ft 11 ½ I was about in the middle. Smithy was shorter and went to 714, I never saw much of him again but always spoke as we passed.

I found myself in a barrack room with about thirty other lads from all over England. Next bed to me was John Sangster from Glasgow called Jock, who lived in the Gorbels, a district on the south bank of the river Clyde. I couldn't understand a word he said at first but we became good friends. Our squad sergeant was Sergeant Wayne, the biggest strongest bloke I had ever seen who towered above us at about 6ft 10 with hands like dinner plates. You didn't mess with him or he would pick you up by your battledress collar with one arm and shake you like a rat.

What followed was sixteen weeks of very intensive training, drill, PT, assault course, long runs and, in between, classroom learning. We had to know all the ranks and badges, Army law, and how to write reports etc. There wasn't a minute to rest, for as soon as we finished for the day we had to clean all our kit. The lights went out at 10 o'clock and we were up again at 6am. Sixteen weeks of total bulls**t. We were thirty lads all with different accents, they called me 'Farmer'.

We tried to achieve an immaculate turnout and helped each other. In the evening, the room would be thick with smoke. I was one of the few who didn't smoke. Jock would be desperate for a fag before payday, which was £1 a week, so I would lend him a bobby (six pence) to buy five Woodbines.

Towards the end of our training we had two weeks motor training, Jock and I in a Morris thirty hundred-weight truck. One had to sit in the back while the other drove with an NCO instructor. We drove all around Surrey and South London. I got on very well having had a jeep because to change gear you had to double de clutch. One day when we got back to barracks the sergeant instructor said by the way you have passed your test with a full licence. Jock failed. When we had weapon training were given very little practise to fire the pistol, Sten gun and .303 rifle. I failed the pistol and Sten gun but came third out of ninety lads with 66 out of a hundred with the rifle. I'd had a rifle of my own.

When our three squads had our passing out parade we were immaculate in our white webbing and red hats all marching in time with our arms swinging at shoulder height, a sight to behold.

While on a forty-eight-hour weekend pass, I was walking up from Cheltenham when I was given a lift by a man who turned out to be Bert Canton from Sheepscombe, my father's teenage friend from when he lived there. He saw my jeep parked up on blocks and offered me thirty pounds for it. I sold it to him and regretted it ever since.

During training we were told we would all be going to Cyprus due to the EOKA troubles, however, when an armistice was signed in February 1959, we were then told we would be staying in England. Coming back from two weeks leave after training, I saw a notice on the Company board asking for six men to go to Cyprus as dog handlers. I said to Jock how about that, and he said let's do it and see a bit of the world. So Jock and I, and another Scottish lad called Harry Profit, went to see the Sergeant Major to tell him we were up for it. He said fine but told us we would have to go on a dog handling course at Melton Mowbray in Lincolnshire, to the Army veterinary core depot. We then, with three others from our intake, took a train to London, through the underground, then on to Melton Mowbray carrying all our kit.

I was given a black Alsatian dog called Carlos, a pussy cat it turned out, compared to the dogs in Cyprus. After two weeks training, then two weeks embarkation leave, the six of us were off to Cyprus. We flew from Blackbushe Airport in Hampshire, on a DC6 piston engine plane, my first time on a plane, landing at Nicosia airport at dusk after a six-hour flight refuelling in Rome. We were collected by a six-ton Bedford lorry, all sitting in the back, where we had our first sights and smells of Cyprus. I can still remember the smells of the roadside Kebab stalls.

Cyprus had a mixed population of Greeks who were the majority and Turks, the minority. The Greeks wanted independence from Britain and union with Greece, the Turks didn't. The Ethniki Organosis Kyprion Agoniston (National Organisation of Cypriot Fighters) EOKA was established in the 1950s and led by General Georgios Grivas, a World War I and II veteran. Driving through what was once mixed villages, every other house was burnt out. The British army spent years trying to find him, but he always avoided capture.

It was a Friday evening when we arrived at Lakatamia camp, sixth army guard dog unit, six miles from Nicosia. We were given a tent by the guard room and told to report for duty Monday morning. A lad came in with a bottle of local wine to welcome us. A thick red wine, a bit like Port, we thought it was very nice and asked him where he had got it from. He told us it was from Lakatamia village. In the morning we wandered down to the village and bought eighteen bottles at 1/6d each, drinking it all day Saturday, by the evening we were all blotto, next day we all felt so ill we never moved from our beds and still felt rough on the Monday morning.

When we went on duty they wanted a driver. Harry and I were the only two who had passed our driving tests. Harry had had a full licence in civvy street, so he got the job and drove all over Cyprus for the duration. I was given a dog called Colonel and when I went with a lead to get him out of his tented kennel he went spare. It took me a week sitting near him and giving him bits of meat before he mellowed down. When I walked up to him, he stood up and wagged his tail, that was the time to go in and put the lead on him. Once dogs were out on a lead they were ok, they just wanted to pull ahead of us. Out of the five of us dog handlers who went to Cyprus I was the only one not to get bitten. Some were bitten quite badly; one having thirty-eight puncture wounds on one arm and was covered in blood.

We were there to guard a 11,000-ton ammunition dump. There was row upon row of half round tin huts, open ended with earth embankments at each end. Boxes and boxes of shells, tank mines, and hand grenades etc. No EOKA ever tried to break in, I think they were afraid of our killer dogs. We would load up at dusk onto a lorry and go to patrol the dumps, it was very boring. Most of us sat against an earth bank with our dog's lead tied up to our elbows, and hands clasped together and dozed. The dog would jump up if there was anything about, mostly large hares, and would let us know if the duty Sergeant was doing his rounds.

On eight occasions, a few of us had to go to Nicosia in full white kit to help patrol with the local Military Police. We carried a pistol but were not allowed to load it, with six rounds in our ammo pouch, patrolling round the city and up Murder Mile where so many of our soldiers and airmen had been shot in the back by cowardly EOKA during the troubles. The Black Watch were in Cyprus at this time and caused a lot of trouble when they were drunk. We would try to get them into a taxi and tell the drivers to take them back to barracks. I never arrested anybody; it saved a lot of paperwork.

One morning, on patrol with our dogs in the Square, we looked up towards camp and saw flames and smoke. We got back, put our dogs away, and found my, Jock and Harry's tent smoking, all that was left was bed frames and a tin wardrobe, I lost everything, including all my civvy clothes. All I had left was the shirt, shorts and boots that I was wearing. They said it must have been a fag end, I said it was not mine as I didn't smoke! We had to go to stores and be re-issued with all new kit, which meant getting it all in order. As it turned out I never wore most of it again.

Shortly after arriving in Cyprus, we heard that we were to be re-allocated to a new camp at Dhekelia on the south coast, everything including the 11,000-tons of ammunition would have to be moved. One day whilst helping to move a lorry load of equipment to the new base I saw a building by the kennels and asked what it was for. I was told that it was the new dog cook house. At Lakatamia the dog cook house was just a tent with a fridge. I asked the MP who worked there if he liked his job, who replied that he hated 'cutting up bloody meat' all day long; so I asked if he would like to swap jobs, to which he replied 'willingly'. The Sergeant Major agreed we could, so after moving into the new camp I went into a brand-new building with my own quarters, hot and cold water, and a very large fridge.

We had in camp up to one hundred and twenty dogs, mostly Alsatians, some Dobermans, and a few Labradors used for tracking. My daily job was to cut up into small pieces a hindquarter of best beef, seven days a week. I was excused all other duties and even had my pay brought to me. Every dog had to have one pound of meat, one pound of hard tack biscuits and some vegetables cut up and mixed and dished out into bowls for their five o'clock feed. I liked the job; it was better than patrolling an ammo dump at night in all weathers.

Sometime after starting the new job in Dhekelia, I was informed one morning in August that my father, who had been suffering from lung cancer, had got much worse and was not expected to live more than a few weeks. I was told that SAAFA, an army charity, had granted me an airline ticket to go home on compassionate leave. I had to go to Nicosia to catch the five o'clock flight, I had to have a passport and civvy clothes as we were landing in Switzerland on the way home and couldn't wear uniform. I was rushed into Nicosia and bought a lightweight coat, trousers, shirt and shoes as I had lost all my clothes in the tent fire. I had to get a photo done and wait at the consulate for a passport.

Flying home on a Britannia aircraft, I suddenly wondered what I was supposed to do when I got to Heathrow, nobody had told me, and I had no paperwork. Coming out of Heathrow I had five and sixpence in Cypriot money and dressed in thin clothes; I was frozen. I thought which way is West, I was going to have to walk home. Seeing a REME soldier in a red beret, I asked if by any chance they were looking for me. He said yes, and that he had to get me to London for the 12:20 train to Cheltenham. We raced across London in an open Champ military jeep, and I managed to catch the train by running down the platform and opening the door as it pulled out, with a travel warrant in my hand. Halfway home, by Didcot, I was very sick, whether it was the airline food, or tension of the day, I don't know.

Arriving in Cheltenham about 2:30 am I found a taxi and asked how much up to Crickley Hill. I said that I would have to knock my mother up to pay, he said that it would be ok. It had been a long day. My father was in Salterley Grange sanatorium, and I sat with him most afternoons until he died, wasting away with lung cancer. He had been a heavy smoker, sixty woodbines a day, and had been gassed in the First World War. Seeing him die like that resolved my intention never to smoke. I had six weeks leave altogether and after the funeral I received a travel warrant to report to a transit camp at Hendon. I travelled in civvy clothes from Heathrow on a Comet jet.

I was in my job at the cookhouse for the next year, now permanent camp staff on duty seven days a week. My work finished by lunchtime, and I could have an afternoon kip, but I had to be there for the 5 o'clock feed. It was too hot to sleep under a net, but you had to cover your mouth and nose because of the flies. Some afternoons a few of us would walk a mile down to the beach to swim in the warm waters of the Mediterranean. There was a fund in the camp that bought various things and you could borrow snorkelling masks and flippers. It was very nice to swim out to sea and see the fish beneath me, which included large Manta ray. Some evenings I would go over to the garrison running track and do four circuits, a mile, to keep fit. I could never persuade any of my mates to come with me.

We spent most evenings in the NAAFI drinking, playing cards and listening to LPs, although we only had three, Frank Sinatra, Shirley Bassey and the soundtrack to the 1956 musical Carousel. No one wanted to listen to Carousel so I used to play it after everyone had left. I knew all the words to the tracks, such as You'll Never Walk Alone.

In the NAAFI, a volunteer dog handler from the tank core called 'Tanky' taught me how to play chess. He played to win, showing me where I went wrong each time, after a few weeks I eventually won a game, then after a couple of months I never lost a game. After a while no one would play me.

Every day the ration lorry brought in a hindquarter beef, frozen solid, which I would put in the fridge to be cut up next day. It was Australian beef, some of it dating from 1942. I also had five 28-pound tin boxes of biscuits sealed with a round lid, also left over from the war years. Sometimes I would find little notes inside, written by the women who packed them. The empty tins and boxes I put out behind my store for a weekly refuse collection and found that all the tins disappeared, so I stacked them inside. The civvy workers came in and said, 'no tins Johnny?'. I said 'yes, 10 mil each!' which was about two shillings. For the rest of the year I had a nice little earner of between ten or twelve shillings a day. It kept me and my mates in beer money very nicely.

After cutting up the meat, always surrounded by flies, I washed the floor and chopping block, and before going to lunch, I walked from end to end with an aerosol fly spray and closing the door behind me, after lunch the floor would be dry, and I could sweep up a saucer full of flies.

One day, Les Cambridge who was in the Signal Regiment at the garrison walked in to see me. I had known him for years; his mother had been one of my teachers at Birdlip school. His wife Marie, the sister of the girl who would later become my wife (not that I knew that at the time), had been a barmaid at the Air Balloon pub, and they lived at Larnaca. Another teenage friend, Ken Bartlett, who was in the Royal Army Service Corps, called in one day driving a Skoda Octavia and said how about coming out tonight to Nicosia. I asked if we could pick up Les and Marie, so we all went to Nicosia, about forty miles away, and went to a night club and saw some belly dancers. This was my only night out in Cyprus. Les asked if I would come and stay with them during my embarkation leave. Larnaca, ten miles from Dhekelia was sandy beaches all the way. I am told now that it is built over with hotels. I had two nights at their house and got a lift back on the ration wagon.

Two weeks before coming home, my job was given to an old soldier called Darkie Endy, a volunteer dog handler from the artillery regiment. He also took over a kitten that a civvy worker had brought me. He came in some days to help me cut the meat up. I later found the place in a right mess, greasy floor and dust everywhere. I wondered how long he would keep the job.

Me, Jock and Harry were taken to Nicosia airport and flew home on a Comet jet. Arriving at Inkerman barracks, we had to hand in our uniforms but I managed to keep my cap badge. I said goodbye to Jock and Harry and caught a train at Woking and came home. My National Service days done. I never kept in touch with anyone but I did bump into a policeman at the Three Counties Show a few years later who I recognised from Cyprus.

The Cookhouse, with a little garden I made at the side

At the beach with some of the lads

Partying with the lads in the NAAFI (Barry and Tanky on my right)

Barry the storeman and Darky Endy unloading a side of beef

Les and Marie Cambridge in Larnaca

Darky Endy (left) with our Greek civvy helper

A week before coming home

THE 60s

Arriving home from my National Service in 1960, I had eighty pounds in Army credits, they made you pay half your wages into a savings account. I owed Les Davis sixty pounds for repairing my motorbike, having come off it during my compassionate leave. I desperately needed a job and a pick-up truck. If I had a pick-up I would have almost certainly gone self-employed.

It took me two years to get established. My mother had a lodger, who was a carpenter working on a house being built round the hill for the managing director of Bryce-Burgess, a factory at Brockworth. He said that they were looking for a labourer on the factory site, so after an interview at the factory I was enrolled on to the maintenance staff. I worked most of the time at Crickley, I built a wall in front of the house and helped lay a concrete driveway and built in a cattlegrid.

In April 1961, the house and garden were finished, and I didn't want to work in the factory. I was offered a job by a small builder, Jim Beard from Coberley. In the meantime I had bought my first pick-up truck, a half ton green Morris 1000. It was at this time that I got together with the love of my life, Ann Beard, Jim's youngest sister, sister to Marie Cambridge who I had stayed with in Cyprus. She became my wife four years later. She asked if I would pick up a wardrobe in town which I did on my way home through Ullenwood. I asked her if she would like to stop a while. It transpired that she had cut my photo out of the Echo, which my mother had put in on my 21st birthday and had hoped I would ask her out. I had known her most of my life as my father and I, and most of the locals, would go to her father's on a Sunday morning for a shilling haircut. There was only one style, short back and sides; we used to tell people he used a pudding basin.

I worked for Jim Beard until November 1962, when I decided to go self-employed. My first job was for Les Davis at the Air Balloon. I built the steps and pillars going up to the lawn area. I had lots of work lined up, when on Boxing Day it snowed heavily for several days covering everywhere three feet deep and more. By then I had traded in my Morris for an A55 Austin Cambridge pick-up (WW0 747). Fitting chains to the back wheels, I managed to get around the main roads. Michael Pye who lived down Dog Lane, who I had been to school with at Birdlip, was a builder and couldn't work. He came up to my house and said that he had a new chain saw and asked that if I cut up some old trees in their orchard could I sell them for firewood for him, going half shares. We did that for three months, buying up trees near the road from various landowners. During this winter the demand for firewood was immense, the snow lasted until April 1963.

My first big job was to build a new corn dryer base and pits for Bill and George Powell at Hartley Farm, the snow was still piled 6ft high on the sides of Hartley Lane. I got the dryer done by harvest time and Bill asked if I would stop on and help with the harvest. They had a Massey Bagger combine that dropped two cwt bags in the field, that had to be picked up and loaded on to a trailer, very hard work. After harvest I helped to plough and plant the whole farm.

November 1963, Heinz Müller sold me an old Marconi television for £1. I took it home and I had an old H aerial which I tied to a line post, tacked a cable into the house, switched it on, it lit up and said there was a news flash, President Kennedy had been assassinated. My mother used the TV for years afterwards.

Ann and I got married on 27 February 1965 in Coberley Church and had a very crowded reception at her house, no 1 Oxford Cottage. The wedding cost me a new suit, 7/6d to the vicar and a few crates of beer, a lot less than some people spend today. We went to stay with Marie and Les in Swindon Rd, Cheltenham for our honeymoon.

I bought a small caravan off her Dad for £85 and Mr Goodrum let me put it on Ullenwood Park farm in exchange for some maintenance work, mowing etc. We lived there for four years exchanging our caravan for a 30ft one after about two years. We had our first son Richard on 25 May 1967, and a second son Simon born on 30 September 1969.

Just after we were married, we bought a lovely Jack Russell puppy we named Sadie, so small she could stand on my open hand. She went everywhere with me, always sitting on the back of the seat. Sadie would bark and growl at anyone that came near the pick-up, but outside she was very friendly. She was a brilliant dog to take shooting, flushing game and rabbits from the bushes and an excellent ratter. One day at Ullenwood camp she killed forty-nine rats. She lived for fifteen years and when she died we were all very sad.

I worked throughout the sixties, soon employing two close friends, Dennis Lewis and Tony Baxter and occasionally Mick Lovelace, the landlord's son from The George Hotel at Birdlip. We undertook all types of work; fencing, gate hanging, stone walling, block laying, concrete bases and driveways, and farm work of all sorts including catching chickens at four o'clock in the morning to load onto a lorry at seven o'clock. Our main employers were local farmers and landowners, such as Mr Dent, Mr Unwin, and Mike Cuttell, and house owners too. We built a Bradstone garage for Mr Sandy Underwood in Coberley. One day whilst working for Mike Cuttell in the Piggery, a young lad called Malcolm working as a pig man, brought out a half-grown dead pig and put it by the muck heap. He had a little side room with an armchair that he would sit in to have his meals. Whilst he wasn't looking Dennis, Tony and I dressed the pig in an old jacket and sat it in the armchair on its haunches, placing an old American helmet on its head and a pipe in its mouth. When Malcolm went for his lunch he opened the door, screamed out loud and ran off down the corridor, it had really frightened him, we all laughed!

Whilst working with Dennis and Tony I carried on my scrap and ornaments dealing, going to most local farm sales. One notable sale was at Winston, when Mr Cove sold up. I bought ten old farm wagons in a field for £6.10s the lot. They were full of straw and thatched as sheep shelters. I dragged them all to one end of the field with the pick-up, took off all the wheels and set fire to them. After a massive blaze, the next day I collected all the scrap metal, and sold the wheels for 30 shillings each for garden ornaments. The best wagon I sold to Colin Paine at Stockwell farm for £10. I towed it away by tying the shafts to the back of the pick-up.

Going to the sales in the sixties led me to make a life changing decision. In 1969, I bought my house, no 2 Oxford Cottage for £2,400 and had possession on the 1st January. My father-in-law Jack Beard, with the help of his son Jim, bought no 1 Oxford Cottage for £1,400, it being cheaper because they had been sitting tenants since the 1930s. I spent the next three months, seven days a week modernising the two houses with the help of my father-in-law and various brothers-in-law. I laid on the water, built a cesspit and drains. New windows to the back, new staircase and bathroom, all new floors, and damp proofed the walls. For the woodwork I employed my schoolmate Arthur Partridge for ten shillings an hour working evenings and weekends. My father-in-law did all the decorating.

To buy the house I had to take out a bridging loan from Barclays bank, I then had to modernise the house before I could get my mortgage from the Halifax. My mortgage was for £1,900. All our savings were gone. In April I had a letter from Barclays bank stating that I had £8 in my account, at the time I owed £450 to Partridges of Birdlip for doing the plumbing work. I went to Ted Partridge and told him that I would pay as soon as I could, it took me until August to pay my debt.

That summer after furnishing the house I hired Bob Cross and Godfrey Daffurn to dig out a large yard at the side of the house with their JCB excavator and tipper lorry. I hired a tractor and trailer from my old employer Jack Garlick for £9 a day. He agreed to have all the soil to level out a field just inside Grove farm.

Over the next two days Bob took seventeen loads down there. I was tipping on Ullenwood Park Farm with the tractor and trailer, filling up old quarry holes. At the end of the first day, I got a puncture in the back wheel of the tractor. I rang Jack who said I would have to get it fixed. I had a tyre company come out who said that there were so many patches it wasn't worth mending. Jack wouldn't pay for a new tube, so I had it patched which cost £8, a lot of money then. I took the tractor back and said that I'd manage without it. Jack rang the next day and said that the tyre was flat again, so I got the tyre company to go out to Grove farm and mend it again, as Jack wouldn't pay £5 for a new tube, costing me a further £8, which was not successful. Jack told me not to bring anymore soil, so we managed to find room for the rest on Ullenwood Park Farm. A couple of weeks later I received a bill from Jack for £17 for tipping seventeen loads of soil. I refused to pay as he had agreed to have the soil to level out a piece of ground for nothing. Over the next few weeks we had several more bills, then a solicitor's letter. Lying in bed one morning I had an idea. I sent him a bill for 17 loads of soil delivered £17.10s. I heard no more from him, and he never spoke to me again, just glowering at me at farm sales.

Ann and me outside the Red Lion pub at Wainlodes Hill
c. 1963 (Cyril Mustoe's Ford Popular)

At the reception with George and Jim Beard, Uncle Sam,
Uncle Bert, Heinz Müller and Sheila Organ

Outside Oxford Cottages with Paul Beard, Heinz Müller,
Jennifer George, Avice Townsend and Margaret Müller

With Sadie outside the caravan

Richard and Granny Beard at the back of Oxford Cottages

*Outside No 1 Oxford Cottage with Gladys and her
granddaughter Gillian Beard*

Ann on a Triumph motorbike

Collecting gravel with Richard at Crickley

Jack and Gladys Beard

In my field with my sheep, Lady, Lenny and cat

ANTIQUES DEALING

By the mid-1970s antiques had become an industry. Thousands of people started collecting, dealing and dabbling, making thousands of pounds and bringing millions into the country. With the arrival of electricity and water in the 1950s to most houses, items such as jug and bowl sets, copper kettles, candle sticks and oil lamps were being put out for the dustmen. In Cheltenham the dustmen would go to Denis Blunt's scrapyard and sell the copper and brass. I bought some nice pieces from him, some for only a shilling. These items were collectable and wanted both in England and the USA and later worldwide. People started to collect anything old, such as radio valves, eye baths, brass blow lamps, cork screws etc. A collector called Mr Bunce in Cirencester had 250 1920s brass and enamel gas cookers in his house. The surge for collecting was helped by the thousands of books published by the subject, one of the first was by Arthur Negus. Auctions boomed, you could go to an auction almost any day of the week. At big country house sales, the London dealers would come down after the Chippendale furniture and Chinese vases. The trade created thousands of job; from restorers, pine strippers, haulers, container packers to shippers.

Having finished the house and moving in on 1 April 1969, I made the momentous decision to give up building work. Tony Baxter had gone to work for Mike Cuttell as a pigman. Dennis Lewis went back to Dowty as a machinist. At this time I had a large shed at Ullenwood Camp, a wartime American Hospital, that I rented off Mike Cuttell, where I stored my building tools and materials including a room full of various antiques, mostly given to me during my building work.

Mr Cuttell senior was always interested in looking at anything I had acquired. I had sold him many stone troughs, staddle stones, oil lamps, china and glass etc. He gave me a lot of good help and advice and even helped me clear a house in Quenington. My first aim was to raise some capital, so I sold a lot of my building materials for scrap etc. In my store I had about thirty old china jug and bowl sets. I mentioned them to a dealer called Jerry Shaw, who said that he would give 30/- each for them. This was my first big sale as an antiques dealer.

I had known Mike Oliver of Tivoli Antiques since I was about seventeen. I had bought some stoneware from him and sold it when it was displayed outside my mother's house. His father Patrick Oliver was one of the top old-school dealers in Cheltenham. He always bought privately, never at auction. When I went with them to look at house contents they only wanted pre 1850 items for their shop and would let me buy the rest which worked out very well for me and gave me a good start to my dealing.

Later that year I took a stall in Roger Champneys Antique centre in Suffolk Road. It was there that I met dealers from all over the UK and abroad. One day I had carried in nine 1920s oak bureaux, the trade said that I would never sell them as they were not old enough. It was a very hot day and I sat there soaked in sweat, when this big man walked in. He said in a foreign accent, "How much de bureaus?" I replied that if he had them all they were £9 each. He said, "Ok, I have them all." The other traders were incredulous calling me an old Jam strangling lucky beggar. This man was Willie Van der Strappen from Holland, his first trip to England, the first shop he came to, I was the first man he bought off. He didn't want antiques; he was looking for good 1920s oak furniture. By this time, I was renting the buildings at Ullenwood Park Farm, and taking him up there he bought loads more off me. He came over to England every two weeks on the ferry, and over the next twenty years or so I sold him thousands and thousands worth of furniture and brass ware.

In my first forays into the house auctions in Cheltenham, I found that there was a ring operating with most of the Cheltenham dealers involved. The ring worked with only one member bidding on an item, none of the others bidding against them, to keep the price down, and they would then knock the items out between themselves later in a van outside. At the large house sales there could be as many as three rings operating. This would cheat auctioneers and estates out of thousands of pounds throughout the 1970s. I have known a set of Georgian chairs making £500 in the sale and knocked out for £5000 afterwards. I found that I had great difficulty buying anything as they made sure that someone would run up the bidding.

One day at a sale in Battledown, I found that there was a tall stranger bidding against me on the stoneware etc. He was not one of the ring, going up to him I realised that he was an American. I asked if he was looking for items like this. He said that he was, and that he was starting up a business shipping containers to California. His name was Charles Whobrey. I asked him to come up to my yard. When he came he said, "God damn it, you have a lot of stuff!" He said that if I could buy for him, he would give me a list of what he wanted and the prices he would pay. This really set me up, I had a small Bedford Luton van painted Heliotrope, the trade called me the Purple Peril, I soon swapped it for a larger Mk1 Ford Transit Luton and started to go out most days buying for Charles. I went to Bristol, Bath, Swindon, Hereford and Worcester, and all over Gloucestershire. Now attending sales, I had a ready market, and I gave the ring hell. They wanted me to join them, but I said no way. I was selling Charles three van loads a week and by the end of 1971 I was turning over £100,000 a year, not bad for a school drop-out. The ring continued to harass me, but I learned all the tricks of auction buying. I remember a sale in Leckhampton Road. I shouted £10 very enthusiastically for an awful very large painted wardrobe, where the ring, thinking I wanted it, bid to £11, I said, "No more." I could hear them arguing afterwards about who was going to take it away.

At most sales it was me versus the ring and most auctioneers knowing this would sometimes knock things down to me very cheaply. I remember Mr Lawson as we walked from one room to the next took my bid on a nice piece of furniture, there was a protest from the ring saying they were going to bid on that, his words were, "I'm in charge of the sale", and then winked at me.

One day at Perry's Sale room there was a nice heavily carved wall clock, and when I outbid Colin the local clock dealer, he took off his beret and stamped on it. I sold the clock to Willie my Dutch buyer.

I took my son Simon to a sale at Moreton-in-Marsh and a very arrogant dealer said to me you won't buy anything here, so I bought every old piece of furniture in the room including a sampler that cost £450. This sampler had everything including, rhymes, cottages, cockerels, numbers and a name and a date, what the trade called 'All singing and dancing'. The dealer from Worcester meanwhile got a parking ticket outside, much to Simon's and my amusement. I put the sampler into my friend Peter Nordan's shop in Burford on sale or return and he sold it for £500 within a few weeks. It always pays to buy a nice item.

One of the old characters in the trade was John Vosper, from Minchinhampton. He had no time for the ring and nobody could outbid him on silver and copper. He would stand at the front of the room and bid until he had bought it. I modelled my buying on him and I could always sell the items at a small profit to my foreign buyers. For about twenty years John always wore the same brown suit, the sort that you were given when demobbed after World War Two, shining down the front from many egg breakfasts.

Throughout the seventies I could sell virtually anything old. I had buyers from America, Holland, Belgium, Australia, France, Italy, Germany and South Africa. When not out buying, I would strip old painted pine furniture in a large caustic soda tank, which I would then wax and polish. I sold some items to June Daybell, who had an up-market clothes shop in the Cheltenham Promenade, for her house at Bisley. House and Gardens magazine did an article about her house and gave me a mention, after which I couldn't cope with the demand for stripped pine furniture. By this time Charles had employed two buyers with lorries so the stripped pine came just in time. I met Charles and Sheila Wye from Stow-on-the-Wold at an auction in Cirencester, they came to me and liked my pine, buying a lorry load every fortnight.

I must mention a friend called Bob Broomsgrove, a retired farmer I met at Cirencester auctions. He and his wife Gwen lived at Sutton Benger in Wiltshire. He also stripped pine and had a stall in Bath Antiques centre. I bought from him and he would buy furniture for me at Swindon auctions. I went to his place every couple of weeks and bought a load from him. Also Dave Brooks from Malmsbury, who had a shop in the town centre, called Cross Hayes Antiques who used to sell me a lot of furniture. I also got to know Mike Thornbury from Malmesbury who started buying furniture from me and is now one of the biggest dealers in the South of

England. Today he buys most of Simon's retro furniture to ship to Japan.

After 1973, with the oil crisis and a Labour government, we had rapid inflation and the price of antiques went through the roof. A Victorian mahogany wind-out table that could be bought for a pound in the sixties was making up to £2000, it was the same with most of the quality furniture, and I needed big money to go to auction. At one stage I had a £15,000 overdraft, there was a lot of bankruptcy around the trade in the 1980s.

My youngest son Simon joined me in the business in 1984 when he was fifteen. The boys had been coming out with me in the lorry from an early age. Simon was very interested in the business and we still work together now. He has become a very skilled furniture restorer. A cabinet maker called Don Gould, who would work for me at weekends, taught Simon and myself about the art of woodworking.

In the 1980s, I had a stall in Ken Shave's Antiques centre in Suffolk road selling pine and display books etc. At one stage, I sold painted effects furniture, much to the amusement of the other dealers. I had gone on a painting effects course at Painswick for two days, me and ten women.

By this time our house clearing service was going full tilt. I cleared houses all over Gloucestershire, and going as far as Bristol, Bath, Oxfordshire and South Wales. From house clearances I collected a vast amount of books, a lot I kept for a my private library. I had to build a first floor extension above my double garage. My main interest was country books, such as the writings of A.G. Street, a Wiltshire farmer, broadcaster and writer of articles in the Farmer's Weekly. I also have a big collection of local village and Gloucestershire History, guides and local postcards.

One of the good things about clearing houses is all the useful things I brought home. I haven't had to buy a light bulb or shoe polish etc. for the last fifty years. My father-in-law Jack was always very eager to help me with house clearances. He was a very keen gardener and picked up loads of tools etc. He would say, "I could do with that", we had many laughs about it.

One of the houses we cleared had belonged to Mrs Aris the old lady who had been murdered in Roman Road, Cheltenham. It was grim, with a lot of blood, and everything covered in finger-print dust. Her small terrace house was so full of bric-a-brac and clothes, and it took a whole week and seven van loads to clear the house and sheds. One day I had both front and back doors open, the wind blew the front door shut so hard that the glass shattered and scattered right across the street. Someone rang the Echo who took a photo of me looking through the broken glass.

Over the last sixty years I must have cleared a thousand houses, and I've been in some spooky old cellars, attics and sheds, it never worried me. However, one day I had a house to clear in Painswick, passed on to me by Roger Champneys. Ann, Simon, Heinz and Paul came to help.

We had a bit of hassle from an old girl next door who said that she had been left some of the furniture which I had to confirm with Roger. We couldn't get it all on the lorry so I had to go back on Monday morning on my own to pick up a few bits. As I walked down a steep path passed a greenhouse to the front door a face looked out of a bedroom window then ducked down. I thought that it was the old girl from next door but then realised that I had the keys in my hand and that the door was locked. The hairs on the back of my neck stood on end, I broke into a cold sweat and my knees turned to jelly. I was really 'fritt'. I had a job to push my legs forward up the stairs but of course there was no-one there. Coming down I picked up a small piece of furniture and walked backwards up the steep path. A reflection in the corner of the greenhouse rose up in the bedroom window, that was it! I've never been frightened like that before or since.

I had a call from Pat Smythe, the famous horse showjumper and author whom I had known when I was quite young. She had been living in Switzerland and had come back to England and bought Sudgrove House after the death of her husband. I had been recommended to her by Aunty Betty Morgan her housekeeper, who was Les Cambridge's Aunty. Pat wanted some bookcases which I found for her. We had a good chat about the old days, and this was the first of many deals she had with me. When she died, I bought from her daughters the remaining contents of her house. In the cellar was a large trunk full of old rosettes she had won. I still have her silver riding crop and some unique horse brasses she had made of her horses Tosca and Prince Hal. I have a collection of most of the books she had written which she had signed and dedicated to me.

In 1978, I bought a brand new Ford Transit Mk 2 Luton van from Bristol Street Motors. The Luton body was made by Johnsons at Toddington. The total cost was just over £5000. I had the van painted with pictures of furniture by a sign writer called Colin Bassett. The van with a V4 engine was rubbish from the start! The engine blew up at 14,000 miles, but luckily I got a new one under guarantee. The last time I used it was from a sale at Gloucester. I left a trail of smoke behind me up Crickley Hill. I scrapped it after just 34,000 miles, but kept the van body for storage.

I have always tried to keep in with the local well-to-do, working for them in the 60s and dealing in antiques from the 70s onwards, I've been in most of the local big houses. Soon after buying the new Transit van I was on the way to Stroud one morning through Buckholt wood. On a sharp bend I met the local hunt coming the other way, all over the road. I stopped, switched off my engine and wound down the window. As they went by it was 'hello John, hello John, thank you John', It made my day.

In 1979 I went to I.D.G. Motors and bought a Peugeot 504 estate car. One of the biggest on the market. I pointed to the car and said to the salesman 'I'll have that one'. Looking at me in my dirty work clothes and shoes he asked how I was going to pay for it. I told him

I'd give him a cheque now and asked when I could pick it up. Doing a quick calculation in his head he said next Friday. When I arrived on the Friday he was all smiles and said 'good morning sir, your car's all ready for you'. My cheque had cleared.

In 1983 my friend Paul Müller told me about a Ford P100 pick-up truck that was coming into Bristol Street Motors, made in South Africa. Put my name on one I said, and I bought one of the first twelve to come into the country. It was written off when someone came round the bend at Salterley on Leckhampton Hill too fast, losing control and hitting me side on. I was taken to hospital and was black and blue but otherwise luckily ok. I have had three more P100's up to 2014, the last one I sold for restoration as they are quite rare now.

Early 1981 I felt quite unwell. I went privately to see Mr Steven Haines, a surgeon. After an endoscopy and a colonoscopy he said I will have you in the Nuffield and put your guts in a bucket to see what's wrong (his words). So I went in for the operation in July where he found a diseased gall bladder which he removed. I lay in bed the next day and watched Charles and Diana get married with my wife sitting beside me. After recovering I was quite fit again. The cost of the operation was £1500, the same operation today would be £10,000 or more. My wife had the same operation in 1984.

I must mention Heinz Müller, a very dear friend for a significant part of my life. He was a German soldier captured by the Americans during the war, interned in

England. Heinz was put to work on a local farm where he met his wife to be, Edna, a local land-army girl. They married and came to live in Ullenwood in the 1950s. They got very friendly with the Beard family. Heinz always called Ann's mother and father 'Mum and Pop', and their children called her Granny Beard. Heinz, Edna and family, Paul, Margaret, Anne and Katie were always the main guests at social occasions. I could always rely on him if I wanted help in the evenings or weekends while my lads were still small. He loved to come out to calls with me and sometimes we would go to Wales on a Saturday buying furniture. Our last night out together was New Year's Eve, 1990. We were invited to the opening of the Kilkenny pub, that I had just furnished for Chris Phillips, and we had a wonderful evening. Just nine days later Heinz died at his daughter's house in Cheltenham, very suddenly from a heart attack. It was a great loss to us all. I did something that I thought I could never do, I stood up and read the lesson at his funeral in Coberley Church. He was so well loved that the church was packed. Anne and her husband Terry went to live in New England USA. Anne took up buying and selling antiques, and I sent them two containers to sell out there and they did very well.

In 1989 I achieved my twenty five year ambition, that was to buy Ullenwood Park farm. Mr Unwin was selling up and gave me first option. I bought the farm buildings and three acres for £42,000. I got a mortgage for £55,000 which covered my costs and overdraft, over fifteen years from Bristol and West. It cost £600 per month.

Throughout the 90s antiques had got very expensive and much harder to sell. You had to buy very carefully. Simon was now self-employed, and worked part time for Wootton Auction rooms, hauling in furniture for the sales. From them we got a lot of house clearances which kept us going.

One of the biggest deals I had in the 1980s was to buy the contents of the east wing of Miserden House. Harry Withers, the estate manager, with whom I had many deals with of metal and stonework throughout the 60's and 70's, called me to give him some prices. Most of the furniture from the house was stored there, including thirty odd metal hot water cans, twenty five jug and bowl sets and some very nice furniture, including a twelve foot pine wardrobe, the biggest I had ever seen. I bought the lot for about £10,000. It was then that I made my biggest mistake; under-selling something. It was a miniature model of a Greek ruin. It was on the floor of my warehouse, and the first dealer to come in was Ken Shave. I offered it to him for £10. He turned it down. The next dealer was Lionel Oliver, who willingly gave me the £10. Some months later I saw something similar on the front cover of the Trade Gazette that had sold for a lot of money. It was a Grand Tour souvenir. When I next saw Lionel I complimented his knowledge and asked how much he got for it. He had taken it to London and sold it for £1,200.

I also bought a lot of furniture from Rendcombe

College. I had got to know Colin Burden, the woodwork master there, and he was in charge of selling the surplus furniture. He became a great friend and we often used to go out together on buying trips, as he was an antiques collector and a part time dealer. Colin rang me one day about some tables that were for sale in Loughborough College in Leicestershire where he had been a student. I went with him and we bought together twenty-nine 9 ft and 6 ft oak refectory tables and forty-five oak benches. We got them all back, with the help of my oldest son Richard, in three loads to Ullenwood by the 1st July. By the 1st of August I hadn't sold one, but by the 1st September I had sold the lot and dealers from all over wanted more. The tables cost £175 each and we sold them for £450 each. One went to New England, and was sold by my friend Anne Willie for $4000, and was later in a New York shop for $12,000.

In the 1980's I met Bob Brown from Portland, Oregon who was buying 1920's oak and ply furniture. After a couple of years buying from me at Ullenwood he asked if I would buy and pack containers for him to save him the expense of coming over. I did three or four containers a year until he retired. It needed about seventy items to fill a container. The lorry would come and we had three hours to load. I would get others in to help, but it was always a rush.

I have always tried to keep on the right side of the law. Two men came to my house on a Sunday afternoon and asked if I would like to buy some furniture. In the back of an old Morris 1000 van on top of a heap of tarmac, they had a very nice French ladies inlaid Bureau and a nice Walnut Sutherland table. They said that they wanted £45 cash for the two. I knew that the Bureau was worth about £250 and the Table about £50 so I said ok. The next day my Cabinet maker Don came in the store and saw them and said what a good buy I had made. That evening he rang me and said that the bureau was described in the Echo as having been stolen from a warehouse belonging to Shires and Lances. The next morning I rang them and told them that I thought I had their stolen items. They came out and confirmed it and took them away, sending me a cheque for £25 as a reward. As I had taken the van registration number the police caught one of the thieves and he got six months. I had a letter from the chief constable thanking me for my honesty. It was a lesson learnt never to buy at the door, something I've remembered when I have had shops. I always say that I will come to look at it in your house.

We have had a few break-ins at Ullenwood over the years, and in 1990 I was given a very vicious Alsatian guard dog called Bobby when a local pig farm went bankrupt. Both Simon and I could manage him but I was bitten twice on my arm and back which was ironic after being the only one during National service not to get bitten. My eldest son Richard couldn't get anywhere near him. In 1994 Bobby was tied up on a long chain to his kennel in my yard when we were broken into by a gang. They beat him up with a piece of wood, injuring an eye. When Simon and I went to work the next day we found him in a pool of blood, unconscious. This gang broke open every door in the place and stole about £5000 worth of furniture and all our electrical tools. Somebody must have told the press and TV and they came for an interview. I had many letters from people enquiring about Bobby. I think that had he been loose they would never had got into the yard, but you were not allowed to have a loose guard dog. Our vet came out and patched him up but he was never the same again and sadly he had to be put down a few months later. This break-in was one of several and was a very big setback for my antiques business. I felt I could never keep anything valuable at my yard in Ullenwood again.

I had been with Colin Burden to Salisbury and bought eight very large staddle stones for £750 from his Aunty. One morning after a very wet and windy night the gate was cut open and the lot was gone, a loss with costs of about £1000. One day I had a visit from some travellers. That evening whilst I was out delivering a wardrobe to Cheltenham, I was gone less than an hour when I got back to find the gate cut open and my Ifor Williams sheep trailer stolen.

At some point in the 1990s most Auctions decided to charge a premium on sales, about 8%. Frazer Glennie was the last of three in Cirencester sale rooms to start charging this. I told them that if they charged me a premium I would never come to their auctions again, and I have kept away ever since. I wanted the other trade to boycott the sales but they wouldn't and now the premium is up to 20% or more which is sheer greed. If a piece of furniture makes £1000 the auctioneers get

£1200 plus, making them £400 and the seller lucky to get £800. Since then I have done all my buying from the trade, private buyers and car boots.

Through 2003 I again had health problems, my left hip had gone wrong, and by the end of the year I could hardly work. I had a hip replacement in Cheltenham General hospital in February 2004 and after two months recovery I was able to work again, these were very hard times with a £600 mortgage. I sold a Grandfather clock out of my house which I had bought in 1970 for £16 and got £2000, not a bad investment, although today it would only make about £250.

Trading changed a lot in the 2000s, with very little export to be had, no containers and very few Americans. We had been going to Sidmouth in Devon a few times for holiday and saw a small shop that was vacant. I took it on a three year lease in 2005. The shop had a flat above and we would spend about ten days a month down there. I employed a very nice lady called Julie Jones to run the shop for me. We called the shop J Ann J (John, Ann and Julie). In the shop we sold bric-a-brac, books and furniture. Simon would come down with a load of restored furniture about every two weeks, and brought back a load to restore that I had bought down there. Sidmouth was a very different market to the Cotswolds, there was still a demand, with the older and retired population, for brown furniture and polished brass and copper etc. They call Sidmouth 'God's waiting room'. We made some very good friends in Sidmouth and still go there once or twice a year on holiday, staying at a flat owned by our very good friends Gerry and Kate Corr. We had the shop for three years until 2008 and afterwards we missed our flat to stay in.

In 2005 I paid off the last of my mortgage on Ullenwood Park farm. It was a great relief to not have to find the £600 per month and to know that I finally owned it. After the shop, the trade went into a very steep decline, brown furniture went right out. Everyone wanted Retro 60s and 70s, mainly G Plan and Ercol, and later almost anything made of teak. At present antiques are hard to sell, only the very best and for a fraction of the price they used to be. Books, glass, china and metalware are unsaleable unless they are useful. About 2010, having about 30,000 books in the store I started to sell online with the help of my daughter-in-law Lucy, she did the computer work, we did the packing and posting. This was quite good when we were selling twenty odd books a week but soon after Kindle readers came out the demand dwindled. This came as a big surprise to the book trade, putting many bookshops out of business. So after about three years we gave up, the online outlets had also got greedy and took too much commission. I still do some book fairs but sell mostly postcards, photos and ephemera. Very few books sell, including local history, which used to be in high demand.

My first attempt to sell away from the store in the 60s was at the puppy show at the kennels in Andoversford. This was long before car boots or antiques fairs had started. China, glass, copper, tools and books sold very well. I did several until the organiser stopped me as I was in competition with their bric-a-brac stall.

When car and lorry boots started at Gloucester market on a Wednesday we were not allowed to open up until 8 o'clock and there would be about 500 dealers waiting, we could sell almost everything we took, those were the days! Since the heady days of the 70s I've done car boots with estate cars, pick-ups and lorries at Cheltenham, Gloucester, Stroud, Leominster, Ledbury, Worcester, Swindon, Burford and at Ullenwood, every year it got harder to sell. If you can make £50 nowadays you are lucky.

We've always called our gear second hand, previously owned or used. At shows some people try to knock you down on price, saying that its shabby or worn. My reply is 'its dead peoples' stuff, what do you expect'. They don't like that and it moves them on.

Every year for the last 30 years we have had a large stall at the Steam fare, first at Kemble and then at South Cerney Airfields. These have always been our best outlet. Buyers there are country people and collectors of cars and tractors etc. Much better buyers than at town car boots. We sell anything mechanical and tools. Enamel signs that I had put away in the 60s costing about £5 or less now make hundreds of pounds.

In 2012 we started to rent a pop-up shop at the top of Bath Road in Cheltenham for a week of two at a time, doing about ten or twelve weeks a year. Although the rent was quite high we always did well. Unfortunately the site was closed for development in 2019.

Smash fright in murder house

WORKMEN GOT the fright of their lives when they accidentally broke the door of the house where 'Little Granny' Constance Aris was brutally murdered in Cheltenham.

Wary neighbours in Roman-road heard the smash and called the police — and officers were on the scene within minutes.

Said Cheltenham removal man John Townsend: "We were moving furniture and old clothes out of the house when we heard an almighty crash.

SLAMMED

"The wind slammed the door shut and the glass broke. That's never happened to me in 20 years."

Cautious neighbours who heard the bang thought it was vandals breaking into the dead Cheltenham widow's home — so they dialled the police.

John Townsend peers through the broken glass in the door.

Said one: "I heard a terrific noise so I went out to see what happened. A police car came down and an officer questioned us. When we told him the door had broken by accident he went away."

A police spokesman would not give any details of the incident except to say: "It was all in order."

Mrs. Aris, a frail 73-year-old grandmother was found murdered in her home in February. She had been savagely beaten around the head with an axe-type instrument.

Her body was found in the living room of her terraced home by her son Dr. Keith Aris and his wife Vanessa the following day.

MANHUNT

Police then mounted Gloucestershire's biggest manhunt, fingerprinting nearly 1,500 people in an effort to trace an isolated print found in her home. Murder squad detectives are still hunting for the weapon used.

At his mother's funeral last month Dr. Aris made an impassioned plea.

"There is still someone out there who murdered her and until that person is found we cannot close the book on her life. I wish the person who is responsible would come forward and put an end to this."

My first P100 after the accident, with the Ford Transit
Mk 2 Luton van in the background

Out for a pub meal with Julie and Barry

My school friend Ian Hoskins in later years

At the pop up shop in Leckhampton on our Golden Wedding

Kemble Steam Fair

Another show

SUMMING UP

I suppose people think things were better when they were young, I certainly do. In the forties and fifties there was almost no plastic and very little waste. Leftovers were fed to the pig. Ashes were used twice then put on the garden. Sugar and flour bags lit the fire. Beer, cider and pop bottles had threepence deposit on them, and were carefully returned. Any that were dumped were rescued by children for the deposit. We made most of our vehicles and everything else you wanted. I used to have a Japanese woman call in who would buy items like tart cooking trays. She would say yes or no as she went through them. When I asked why no, she said that she only wanted those that said made in England, 'no Chinese rubbish'.

Since I started driving, I've had a few vehicles, a jeep, 3 motor bikes, 8 tractors, 9 pick-up trucks, 4 Luton vans, 4 estate cars, a Morris 1100 (for my wife) and a VW Golf 5 door that I bought in 1994 and still use to this day.

We have had some good holidays. Renting a cottage from a local dealer, Beryl Giles, we stayed in Newport, Pembrokeshire, Wales several times, with our boys and Marie, Les and David. Later we went touring North Wales with Edna and Heinz. The year I had my first new pick-up, Ann and I decided to go to North Wales. It was a Sunday and I drove until the afternoon in pouring rain as far as Lake Bala, looking for somewhere to stay. We saw a large hotel on the hill and decided to book in there. When we went in we noticed it was all hunting and fishing and Ann said that we can't stay here it's too posh. I said I've got plenty of cash on me. We didn't enjoy the stay. It was antiquated with noisy plumbing, one bathroom and the guests were all 'stuffed shirts'.

Later that year Ann and I drove the pick-up to Scotland, we had booked into Ladbrooks at Moffat. They told us that if we freewheeled with them we could stay at any one of their hotels in Scotland. So we stayed in Fort William, Inverness, Wick and Livingstone. In all, two very enjoyable weeks. Fantastic scenery and welcomed wherever we went.

Ann and I flew to America in Autumn 1992 to stay with Ann and Terry Willie, the daughter of Heinz Müller, in Fairfield in New England. They took us to New York which was awesome, had lunch at the Waldorf Astoria, an enormous cheap meal, and toured New England. We went again in spring 1994. Halfway across, there was an announcement that the plane had lost the use of one engine and that we were going to divert to Goose Bay in Canada. We were taken to the sergeants' mess and given a meal and free drinks. We arrived in New York about six hours late in the middle of the night. Terry was waiting at the airport all that time and couldn't find out what was wrong, he was very worried. It rather put us off flying.

When the boys were about eight and ten I took them with Les to North Wales and we camped on a farm near Lake Bala for a few nights, cooking our meals on a camp fire. In later years we have been going to Sidmouth, as its only one and three quarters hour drive.

My eldest son Richard also followed a similar path to me but not in the antiques trade. He went to Pates Grammar school, which he did not particularly like, and in 1983, at sixteen, he left. After working on a farm for Mr Dent during the summer, he then went to work for my brother-in-law Jim Beard in the building trade until Jim retired, before going self-employed as a general builder and dry-stone waller. But in 1992 he decided to go to University to follow his interests in Archaeology and also Building Conservation. Later in his forties he decided to give up his building work and went to work first for Cheltenham Borough Council then later Stroud District Council in the Building Control departments as a chartered surveyor.

Our shared interest is growing organic vegetables, which we do together at weekends and summer evenings in the garden behind the store at Ullenwood Park farm. I mainly do the digging and weeding, whilst he does the planting. We've grown some good crops of potatoes, beans, carrots, parsnips etc. and in the greenhouse, cucumbers and tomatoes. There is nothing to beat home grown organic vegetables.

I have recently been able to find 'Walker's seedlings' which I found out were renamed as The May Queen. According to an internet site Richard discovered, it is one of the most popular potatoes cultivated in Japan having been exported there in 1908 by a Baron Ryukichi Kawata. In Assabu, a town in the northern Japanese island of Hokkaido, it is grown so often that the May Queen is the town's mascot. We now grow a small crop every year.

In October 2012 I went to Emerson Green hospital in Bristol and had my right hip replaced. Much quicker than in Cheltenham General, only two days in hospital. In 2018 I had a pain in my chest and went to casualty in Cheltenham, they kept me in and then sent me to the Bristol Royal Infirmary for ten days. I was told that I had an ulcer on my aorta but they did not operate. I am waiting for a scan in 2021.

As I write this we have just come out of a second lockdown from Covid 19. The first one in March, I think was the most idyllic time I've known. Sunny and warm, the birds singing, we sat out in the garden a lot. There was very little traffic and no litter on the roadside. I got my garden planted early and had one of the best crops I've seen.

I am now 82, I think that I am lucky to have got this far. I don't regret anything that I have done. Walking out of school, doing National Service, marrying Ann and deciding to be an antiques dealer was the best thing ever.

Picking beans in the garden, c. 1990. We used to grow a large crop of potatoes!

Ann in a caravan in Bournemouth with Marie, Les and their daughter-in-law Helen

With Heinz and Edna Müller on holiday in North Wales

At our nephew Dave's wedding to Helen

APPENDIX

Eli Walker outside Yew Tree Cottage

My grandparents Thomas and Sarah Hawker

Harry Townsend in PSC uniform (Standing, five from left)

Birdlip School, 1947

My first jeep

Charlie inside the Air Balloon Inn

715 Squad.   'A' Coy.   ROYAL MILITARY POLICE   Depot and Training Establishment.   November, 1958

James C.   Childs P.   Smith E.   Dart A.   Thompson R.   Smith G.   Townsend J.   Abraham C.
Sellwood P.   John D.   Sangster J.   Cooke B.   Barker M.   Gill B.   Bannister K.   Jones B.   Walter R.   Sutton K.
Shrimplin J.   Coulson J.   Newcombe B.   S/L/Cpl. Ayres T.   Sgt. Warne L. (S.I.)   S/L/Cpl. Perkin C.   Fowler G.   Prophet H.   Trumper A.

Colonel

A visit by the head of command Middle East to my dog cook house

Wedding to Ann, with family outside Coberley Church

*Mother and wife Ann with Richard and Simon outside
Yew Tree Cottage in the early 1970s. (Charlie inside)*

Simon and me landscaping the garden

*Colleen, Ramon, myself and Ann outside
the store in Ullenwood*

Our shop in Sidmouth

At a fair with Ann and Marie

Ann and me

ACKNOWLEDGEMENTS

Over my antique career I have met many people, some no longer with us. I would like to thank all those that have worked for me, and have become friends: Don Gould, Roger Slinger, Chris Pulford, Simon Thorn, Chris Johnson, Alan Davies.

All the dealers from abroad: Charles Whobry, Willie Van der Strappen, Robert Ryceart, Tom Kramer, and Bob Brown.

English dealers: Mike Oliver, Roger Champneys, Ken Shave, Martin Light, Dave Kent, Bob Bromsgrove, Mike Thornbury, Nigel Dimmer, Brian and Nigel Moss, Tom Anderson, Alan Ponsford, Martin Wheatley and many others.

Dave Gillet, Heinz and Paul Müller, Ann and Terry Willie, Peter and Jenny Nordan, Colin Burden, Dave Newman, Peter Jenner, all good friends.

Above all a big thank you to my two sons Richard and Simon. Richard who is married to Lucy and gave us two beautiful grand-daughters, Esme and Clara. Simon who has kept me company in the antiques trade and for keeping the house and garden up together. And to my wife Ann, for looking after me in sickness and health.

The author at Berkeley Show